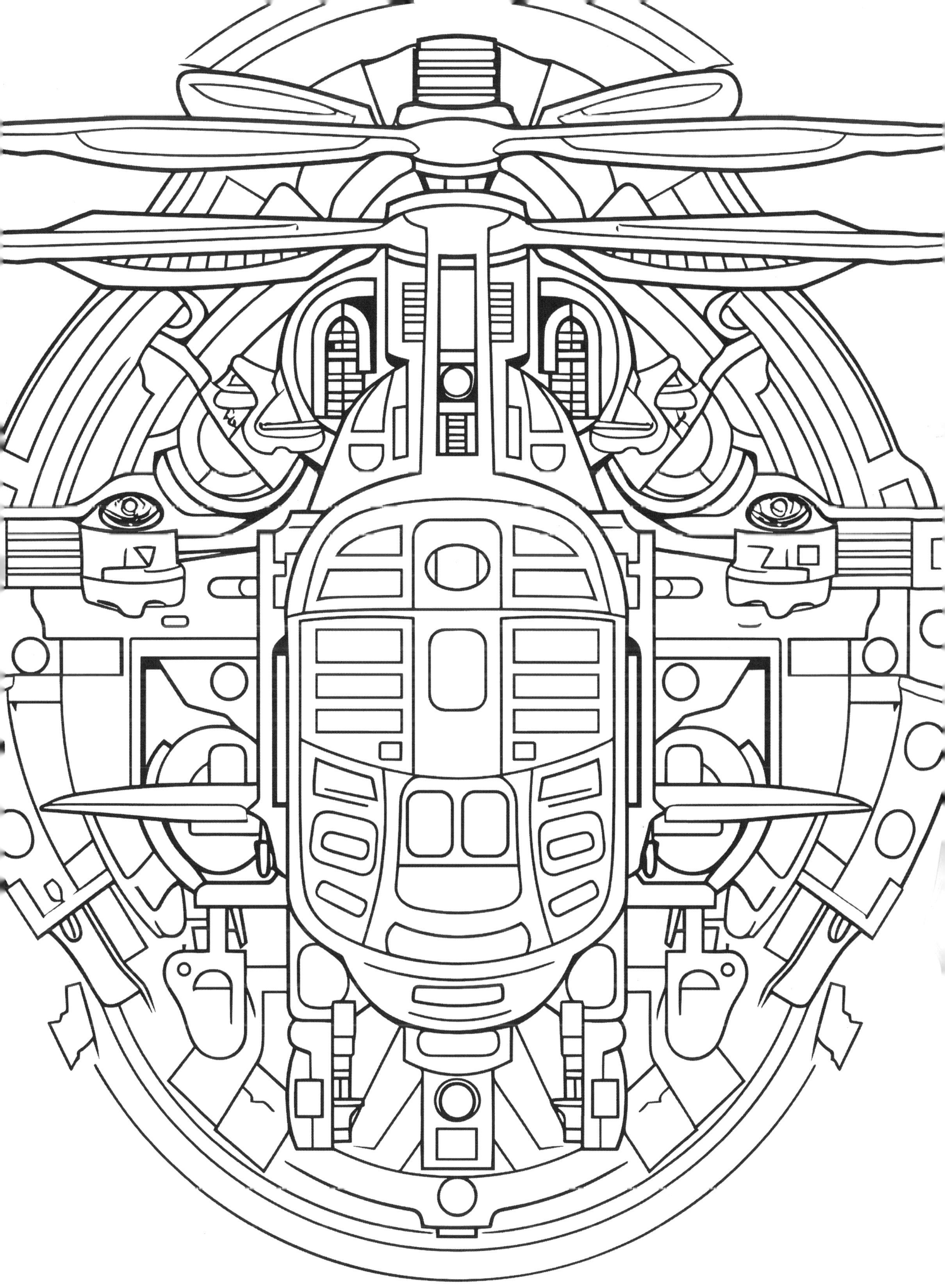

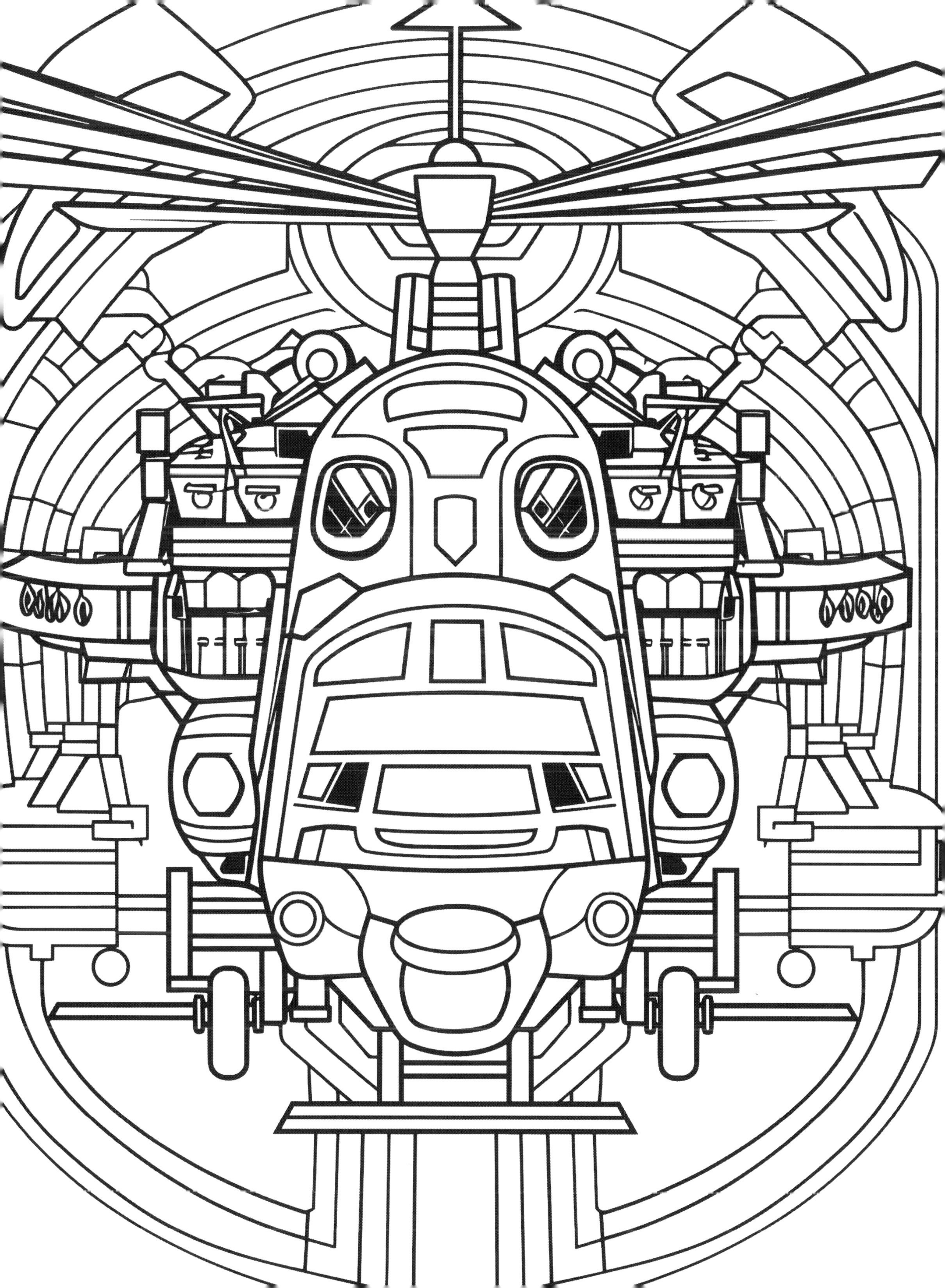

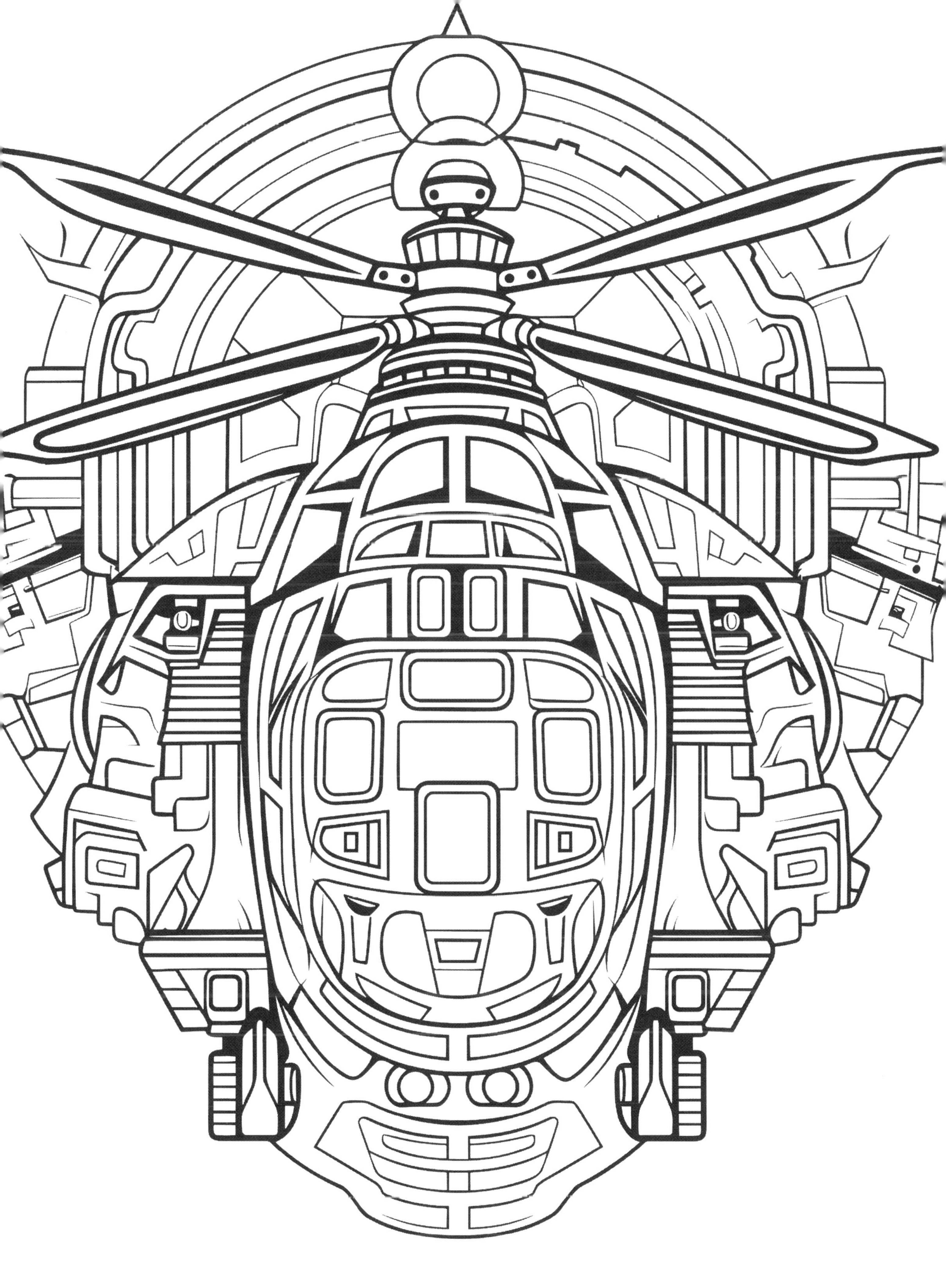

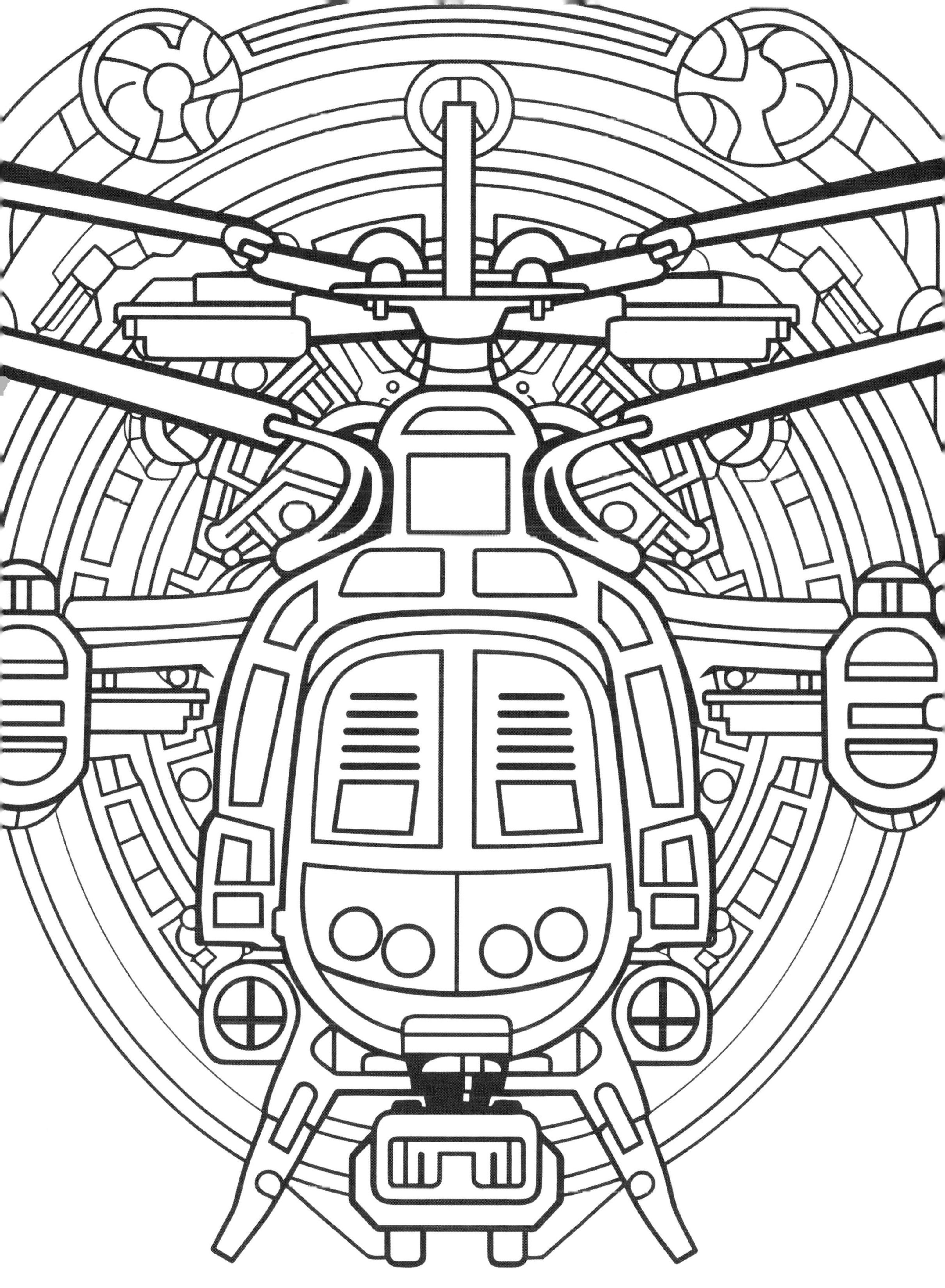

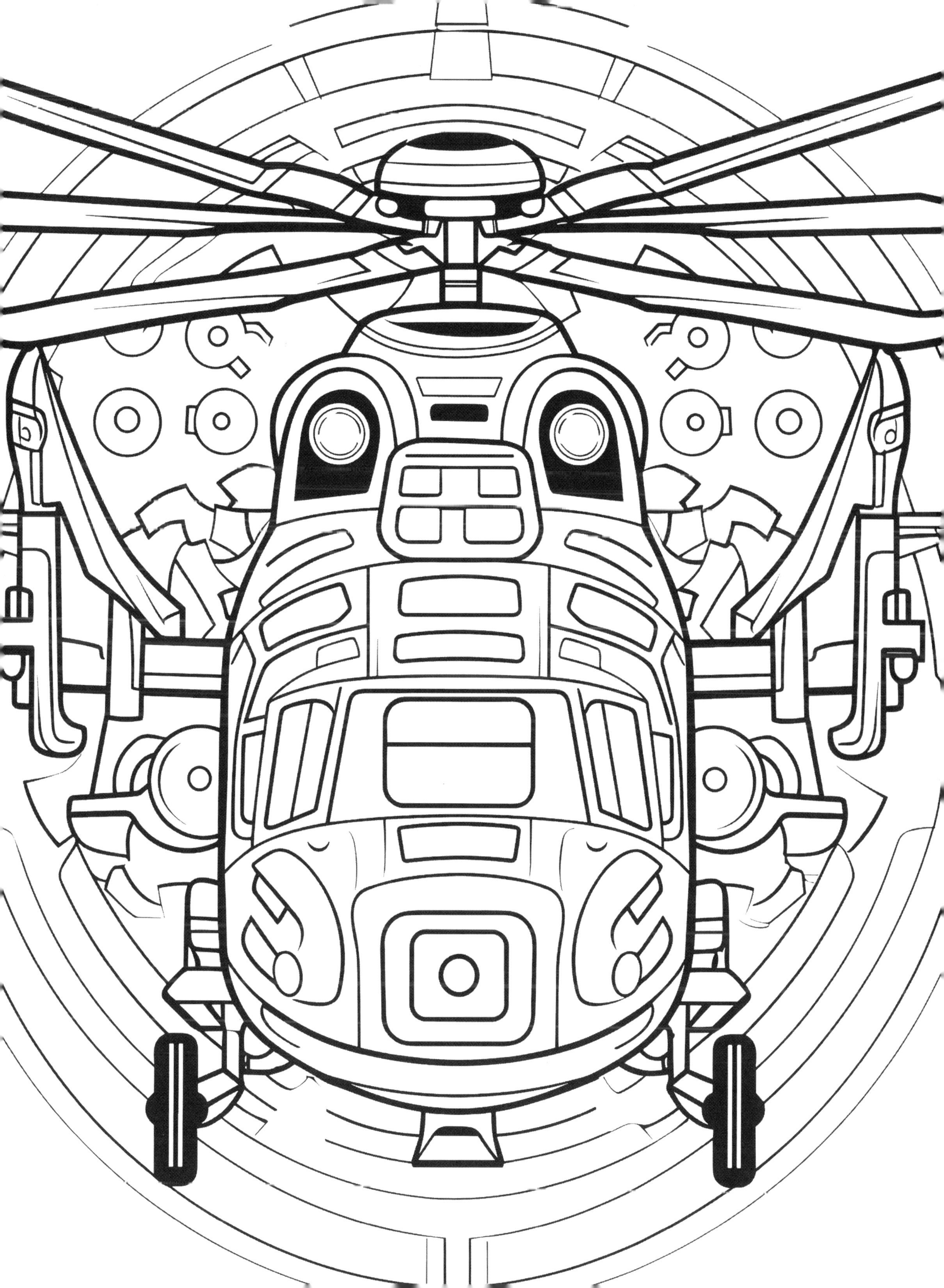

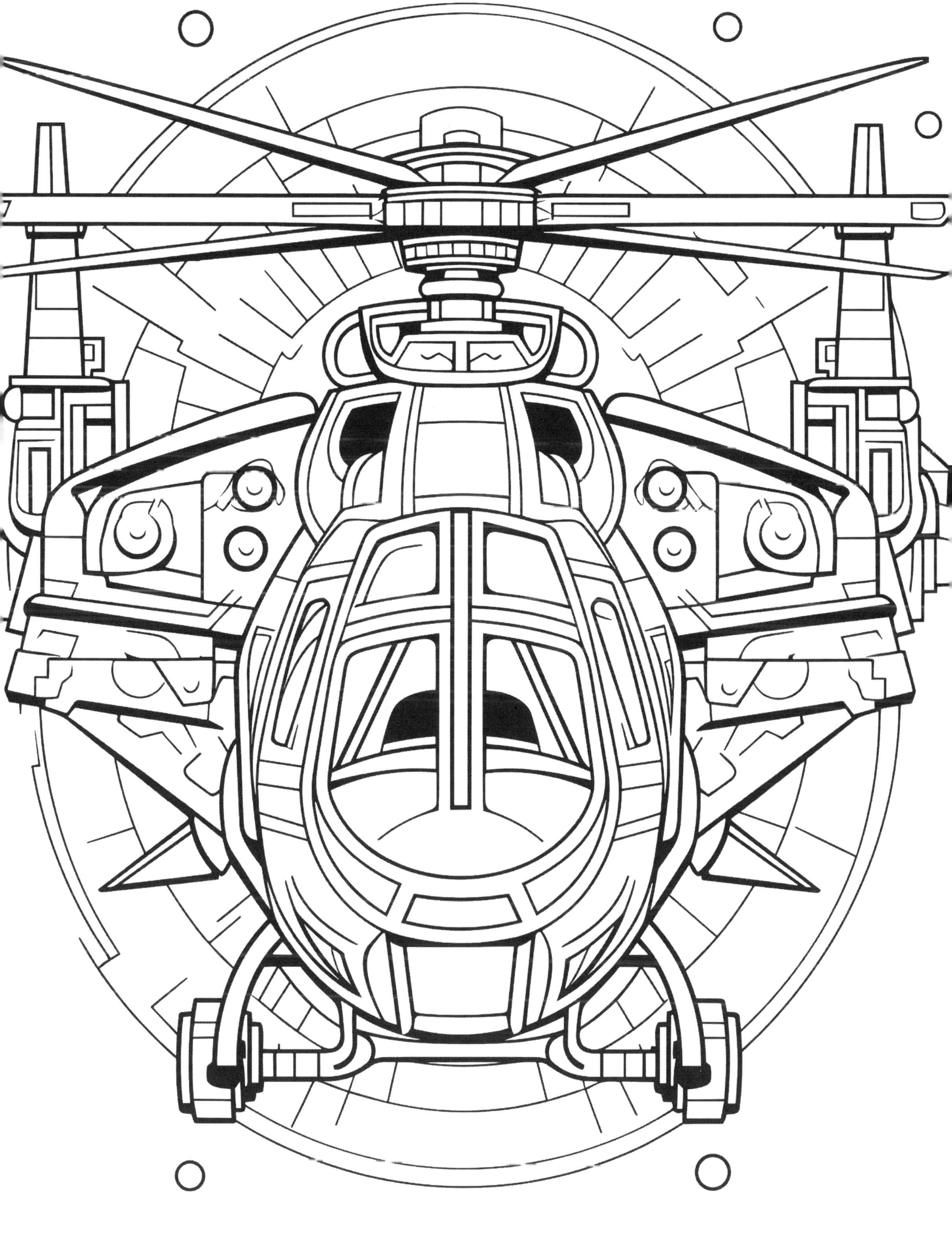

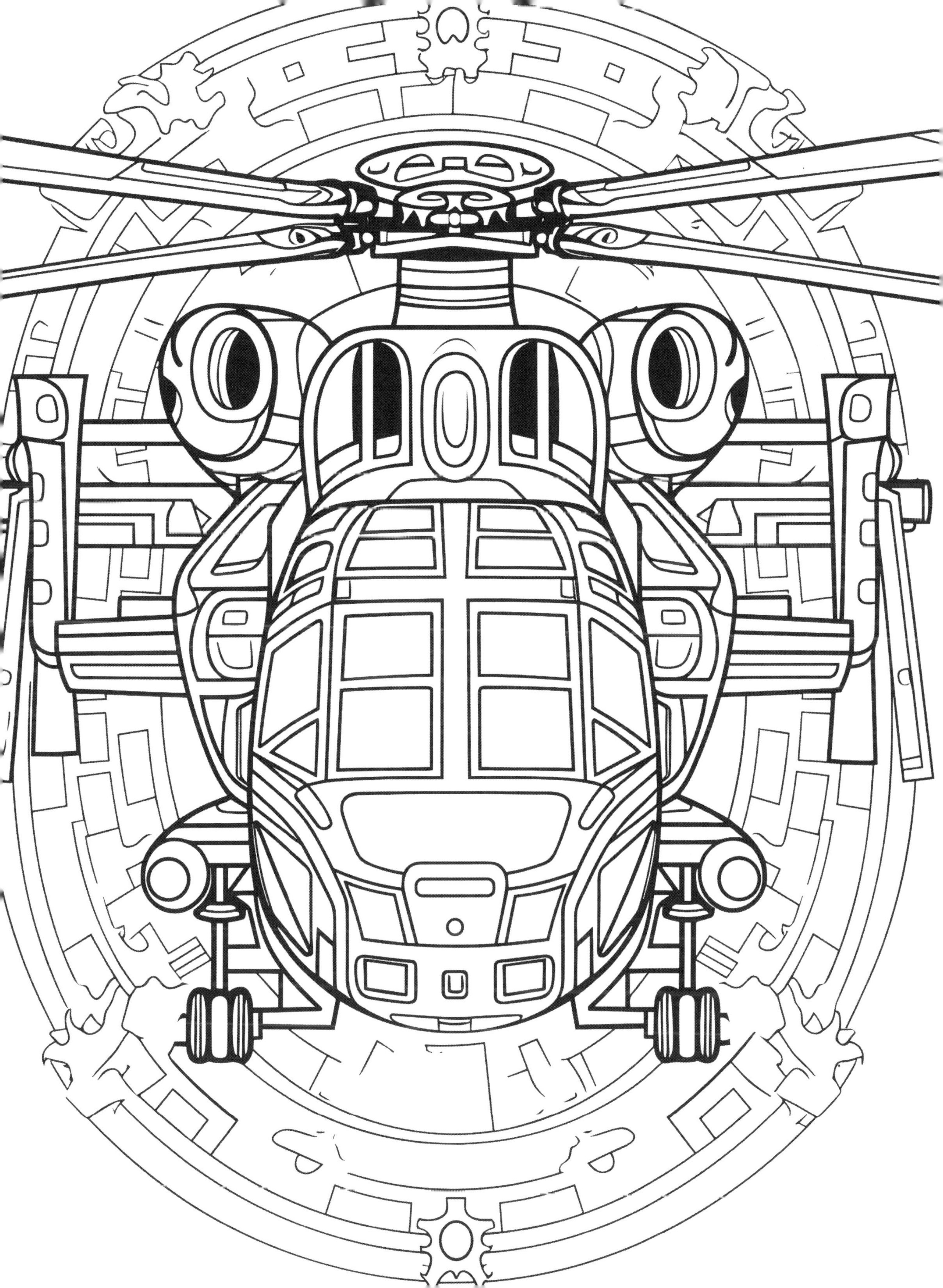

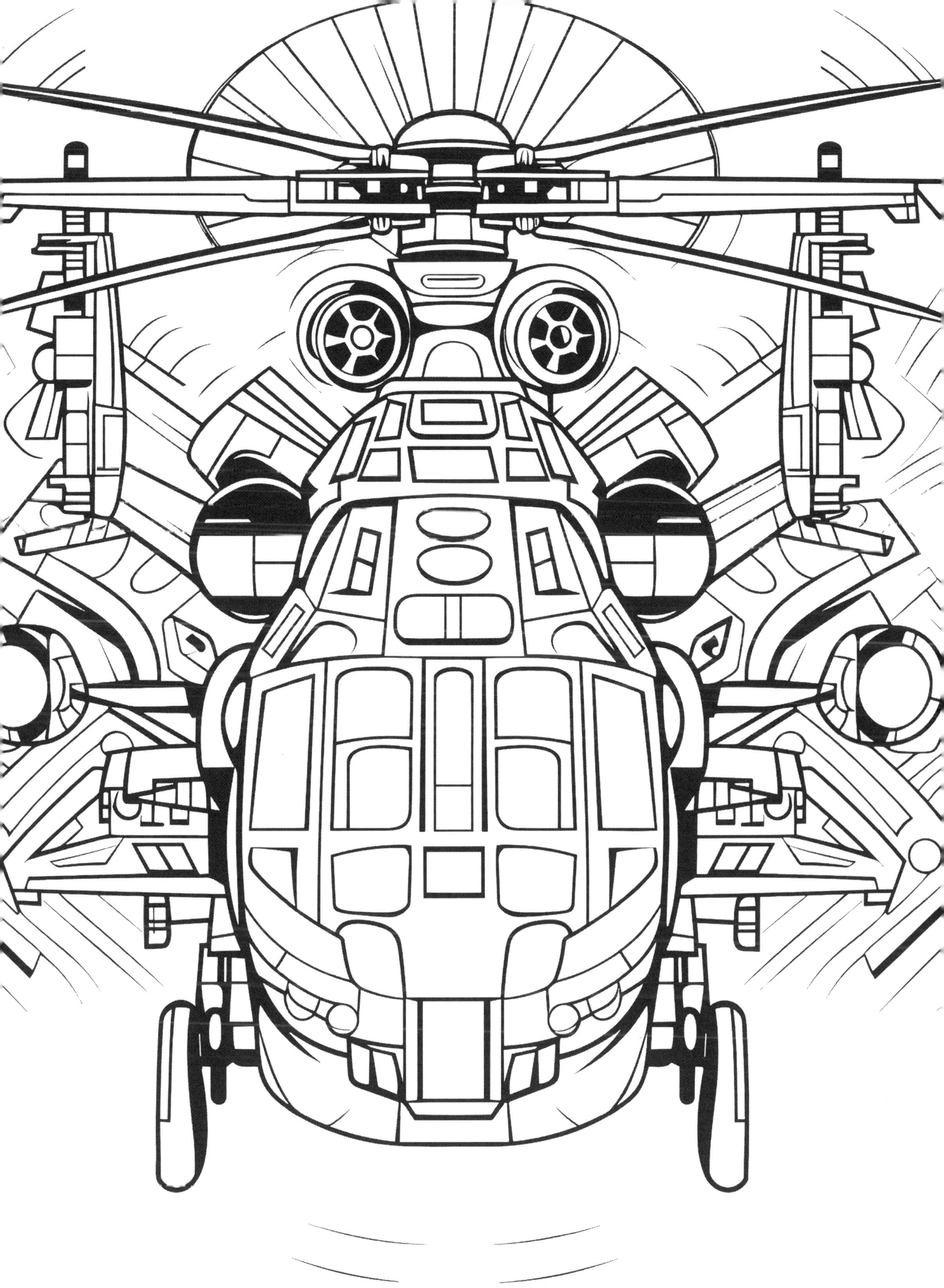

Made in the USA
Columbia, SC
04 February 2025

53255489R00046